When I grow up, I'm going to play for...
REPUBLIC OF IRELAND

Written by Gemma Cary
Illustrated by Tatio Viana
Designed by Sarah Allen

First published by Hometown World in 2016
Hometown World Ltd
7 Northumberland Buildings
Bath BA1 2JB

www.hometownworld.co.uk

Copyright © Hometown World Ltd 2014

ISBN 978-1-84993-777-1
All rights reserved
Printed in Poland

10 9 8 7 6 5 4 3 2 1

Soon Jack found himself outside, standing in a puddle. What was he meant to do out here? His football was flat and there was no one to play with.

On the back of his bedroom door, Jack found what he wanted: his Republic of Ireland shirt.

For some reason, he always felt more confident wearing this shirt, and he usually played better, too. He put it on and instantly felt happier.

Just then, Jack heard the familiar thump of a car door.

"Hello, Mrs Bettershed," called Jack's dad, appearing in the back garden. Mrs Bettershed glowered and speared the tennis ball with her hefty pitchfork. "Sorry," said Jack, trying not to laugh.

"Hello, Superstar!"

Dad held out a bag and Jack peered inside. It was a brand-new football! Not only that — it was in the colours of the **Republic of Ireland** football team.

"Cool!" said Jack.
"We're celebrating," said Dad, "because today is the first day of the new season!"

The pair were soon having their best-ever game of football. They seemed to play for hours!
When they eventually stopped for tea, Dad said, "I've spoken to our team and they're having a trial tomorrow. They said you can come along, if you want to."

Next day, father and son arrived at the football grounds. The changing rooms bustled with children in blue and red bibs, nervously waiting to show off their skills.

But secretly, Jack was worried about his own performance. When the half-time whistle blew, he had barely touched the ball, let alone scored.

Someone near the subs' bench caught Jack's eye. It was his dad, waving madly. Jack jogged over and his dad pulled the Republic of Ireland shirt from a rucksack.

"Wear this under your bib, Son. You always play brilliantly with this on."

Jack did as his dad said. As he sprinted back onto the pitch, he imagined he was stepping out of the tunnel at the Aviva Stadium. Flags rippled through the air while the crowd sang the national anthem.

All of a **sudden**, Jack was the best player on the pitch! In the second half he scored three incredible goals, while no one else scored more than one.
He was confident. He was happy. He was ...

At the end of the trial, the coach called out the names of players who had made the final eleven: "Danny, Olly, Leo ..."
Everyone clapped after each name.
"Joe, Sam, Joshua ..."

Jack leaped into the air, waving his arms in excitement.

"I'll take that as a 'yes'," said the coach, and everyone laughed.

Dad couldn't stop grinning. He praised Jack all the way home. "You were amazing, Son! Unstoppable. A real champion!"

"Cheers, Dad," Jack replied. "I can't wait for my first match. But one day I suppose I won't be able to play for them any more."

"Oh? Why not?" asked Dad.

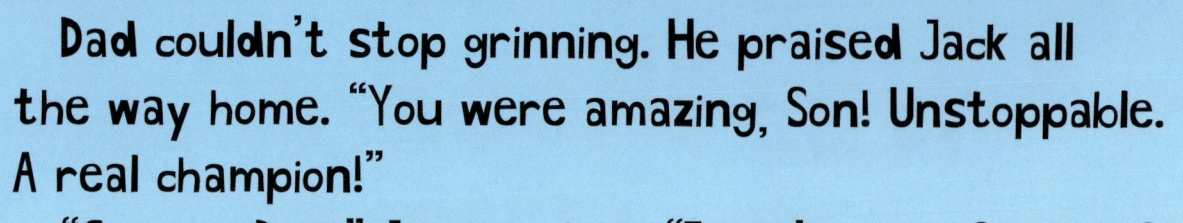

"Because when I grow up, I'm going to play for

Republic of Ireland!"

And guess who else is going to play for Republic of Ireland?